MW00445173

THE  COOK BOOK

vegemite.com.au
f VEGEMITE
◎ @VEGEMITE
𝕏 @VEGEMITE
▶ VEGEMITE

THE VEGEMITE COOK BOOK

PROUDLY MADE IN AUSTRALIA SINCE 1923

Favourite recipes that
Taste Like Australia

PENGUIN BOOKS

CONTENTS

THE VEGEMITE STORY

VEGEMITE isn't just owned and made in Australia;

IT TASTES LIKE AUSTRALIA.

The History

The VEGEMITE brand has a history spanning an entire century. In February 1923, the Fred Walker Company, a Melbourne-based food production and export company, hired a young chemist, Dr Cyril P. Callister, to develop a spread from one of the richest known natural sources of B vitamins: brewer's yeast. After months of conducting laboratory tests, Dr Callister developed a tasty spreadable product that was labelled 'Pure Vegetable Extract', which became known as VEGEMITE.

VEGEMITE is now proudly owned by Bega Cheese Limited, the Great Australian Food Company. Bega Cheese Limited purchased the VEGEMITE brand in 2017, bringing it under Australian ownership for the first time in more than ninety years. VEGEMITE is proudly made in Port Melbourne, Victoria.

VEGEMITE's Mitey one hundredth birthday is on 25 October 2023.

the VEGEMITE cookbook

The Spread That Could

The Fred Walker Company was delighted when Dr Callister presented his newly invented spread to them in 1923. They initiated a nationwide competition to pick a name for the new product, offering an attractive £50 prize pool for finalists. Unfortunately, the name of the winning contestant was not recorded, but the winning name of the spread – VEGEMITE – was chosen by Fred Walker's daughter out of hundreds of entries.

In late 1923, VEGEMITE graced the shelves of grocery stores and chemists across Australia. It came in 2-ounce (57-gram) amber-glass jars with a red-and-orange label. 'Delicious on sandwiches and toast, and improving the flavours of soups, stews and gravies' was how it was first described and marketed.

At the time, Marmite (a thick, dark English spread) already dominated the Australian market and Australians were reluctant to even try Fred Walker's locally made product. Poor sales of VEGEMITE resulted in its name being changed in 1928 to Parwill. Walker was determined to emulate the success of Marmite and the logic behind the re-branding strategy was simple: 'If Marmite . . . then Parwill.'

Walker's innovative method of marketing was, however, unsuccessful. Parwill failed to gain momentum across the country. It would take Fred Walker a couple of years of perseverance and a change back to the original VEGEMITE brand for Australians to embrace what would eventually become a national icon.

'VEGEMITE was well and truly a part of Australia's history – and its heart'

The Spread That Did

In 1937, still struggling to find widespread success for VEGEMITE, the Fred Walker Company came up with another competition, this time calling for limericks to promote the brand. The competition offered substantial prizes, including Pontiac cars, which

Cyril Callister

encouraged entries, and also increased sales of VEGEMITE nationwide. The VEGEMITE brand gained official product endorsement from the British Medical Association (the largest professional medical association in Australia at the time). Medical professionals and baby-care experts were even recommending VEGEMITE as a vitamin-B-rich, nutritionally balanced food for their patients. By 1942, exactly nineteen years after it was first developed, VEGEMITE had become a staple product in most Australian homes.

During the Second World War, the Australian Defence Force bought VEGEMITE in bulk, due to the product's nutritional value. In order to meet this increased demand, the Fred Walker Company had to ration VEGEMITE on a per-capita basis across Australia. It's said that absence makes the heart grow fonder, and once the Second World War had ended, VEGEMITE was well and truly a part of Australia's history – and its heart.

The Spread We LOVE

There aren't many products or brands that have been embraced with the same amount of love as VEGEMITE, and even fewer are capable of retaining that love for as long as VEGEMITE has. Did you know that in 2016, Cook Street in Port Melbourne, Victoria (the home of the factory where VEGEMITE is produced) was renamed VEGEMITE Way to celebrate the iconic brand?

The world may be constantly evolving, but one thing that remains steady is Australia's unwavering love for VEGEMITE. And what makes VEGEMITE so great? It's woven into the fabric of our nation. It isn't just owned and made in Australia; IT TASTES LIKE AUSTRALIA.

the VEGEMITE cookbook

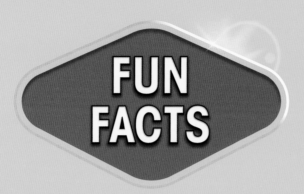

FUN FACTS

- The 'Happy Little VEGEMITEs' song was written in 1954 by Alan Weekes.

- Ever wondered why, when you open up a new jar of VEGEMITE, it's so smooth? It's because VEGEMITE gets filled into its jars hot.

- Whether you're coeliac, low FODMAP, vegetarian, vegan or looking to reduce salt from your diet, there's a VEGEMITE product just for you.

- VEGEMITE is a versatile flavour and can be added to almost anything, including ice cream!

- VEGEMITE Squeezy was created to make cooking with VEGEMITE easier!

- VEGEMITE contains vitamins B1, B2, B3 and folate. B1 is essential for brain function. B2 supports your nervous system. B3 is essential for energy release. Folate helps fight fatigue. Enjoy VEGEMITE as part of a balanced, varied diet and active lifestyle.

- VEGEMITE is best stored in the pantry or cupboard.

VEGEMITE Packaging

Since its debut in 1923, VEGEMITE's packaging has evolved over the last 100 years.

1923 | **1928**

1944 | **1946** | **1952**

1992 | **1996** | **2000**

the VEGEMITE cookbook

1930   1939   1940

1963   1965   1989

2013   2020

Who knows what the future holds for the humble VEGEMITE jar?

THE SONG OF AUSTRALIA

In 1954, a group of bright, energetic youngsters burst into song on the radio to a toe-tapping jingle named '**Happy Little VEGEMITEs**'. Two years later, the infectious tune was developed into a television campaign, which continued intermittently through to the late 1960s. It wasn't until the dawn of the 1980s that the original '**Happy Little VEGEMITEs**' commercials, re-mastered and colourised, returned to Australian television screens to replant a rose in every cheek. The advertisements were broadcast to a new generation of Australians, who revelled in the VEGEMITE brand's nostalgia. The '**Happy Little VEGEMITEs**' commercial was released again in 2010, reminding Australians of their love for the iconic brand and cementing the song's status as an unofficial national anthem of Australia.

a few happy little VEGEMITEs

the VEGEMITE cookbook

HAPPY LITTLE VEGEMITES

We're happy little VEGEMITEs, as bright as bright can be,
We all adore our VEGEMITE for breakfast, lunch and tea,
Our mummies say we're growing stronger every single week,
Because we love our VEGEMITE, we all adore our VEGEMITE —
It puts a rose in every cheek!
We're growing stronger every week!

VEGEMITE IN THE SECOND WORLD WAR

VEGEMITE becomes an Aussie staple
during the Second World War.

During the first twenty years of its existence, VEGEMITE struggled to capture the Australian market. However, during the Second World War VEGEMITE became the beloved Australian brand that we know today.

In 1939, VEGEMITE was endorsed by the British Medical Association (Australia's largest professional medical association at the time) and embraced by the Australian army, which purchased the spread in bulk for Australia's armed forces during the Second World War.

Professor Cedric Stanton Hicks was commissioned by the Australian government to ensure that Australian troops were receiving adequate nutrition while serving their country and, after extensive research, Hicks concluded that VEGEMITE, a rich source of vitamin Bs, should become the basis of soldiers' ration packs, along with blackcurrant concentrate and margarine. 'Hicks sent VEGEMITE to war and that transformed its status,' says Jamie Callister (author of the book *The Man Who Invented VEGEMITE* and grandson of VEGEMITE creator Dr Cyril P. Callister).

the VEGEMITE cookbook

As the Second World War unfolded, VEGEMITE became closely associated with national interest and the war effort. The distinctive jar appeared on posters throughout Australia, bearing the slogan 'VEGEMITE: Keeping fighting men fighting fit'.

To ensure there was enough VEGEMITE to service the Australian troops, it was rationed on the home front, with civilians limited to a per-capita portion. Following this shortage, product sales increased and by 1942, VEGEMITE had become a staple food in Australian homes. Its reputation as a distinctively 'Australian' food would continue to grow throughout the rest of the twentieth century.

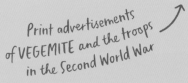

Print advertisements of VEGEMITE and the troops in the Second World War

"Vegemite" Makes Nicer Sandwiches and Soups

"Vegemite" gives just that niceness that makes your Sandwiches, Soups, etc., a source of pride to you and a pleasure to your family.

"Vegemite" is a pure vegetable extract, containing the vitamins so necessary if you are to get the best out of your food. It is good for you, and the children will certainly thrive on it.

"Vegemite is Economical"
Only a little "Vegemite" is needed. Use it sparingly. It is much nicer this way.

Vegemite
THE WORLD'S WONDER FOOD

Sold by Chemists and Grocers in 1 oz., 2 oz., and 4 oz. Amber Jars.

30s

The Vital Substances ...in Food...

EVERY MOTHER SHOULD KNOW

that in much otherwise good food the vital substances, vitamins, are lacking, and children cannot thrive without these vitamins. Such food becomes entirely wholesome and nourishing if the vitamins are supplied to the system.

VEGEMITE, the Wonder Food of the World, contains the vitamins and completes all other foods. Only a little is needed to balance perfectly each meal, and make it what every meal should be — a pleasure in itself and a means to continuous health, strength and happiness.

Make VEGEMITE part of the daily food of your family, either in the form of sandwiches, which children specially like, as a thin spread on bread or biscuits, or added to soups, stews and gravies.

Vegemite
THE WORLD'S WONDER FOOD

VEGEMITE is a pure vegetable extract. It is sold by Chemists and Grocers in 1 oz., 2 oz. and 4 oz. amber jars. With each jar there is a useful little book of recipes.

For Restoring the Roses to their Cheeks

Invalids and convalescents need tempting in the matter of their food, and the food must also possess the highest building-up properties. Vegemite, because of the Vitamins it contains, is the food to do this, and its deliciously piquant flavor makes it a favorite with invalids and convalescents.

This is a jar of Vegemite, the Vitamin vegetable paste, for use in Sandwiches, Soups, Stews and Gravies. It is full of vitamins and very nourishing.

ONLY A SUGGESTION IS NEEDED

Only a suggestion of this wonder paste is needed in soups, stews, gravies, sandwiches or in biscuits to make them more appetising and much more useful in the building-up of a good sound constitution.

Vegemite
THE WORLD'S WONDER FOOD

Sold by Chemists and Grocers in 1 oz., 2 oz., and 4 oz. Amber Jars. Save money by buying the 4 oz. jars, which cost less proportionately.

← Early VEGEMITE advertisements were on simple black and white print and focused on adding VEGEMITE into soups, stews, gravies and sandwiches.

50s

40s

You often starve on a full stomach

– for the Vital Vitamins B₁ B₂ and PP

Most people don't realise they're not getting enough of these vitamins into their diet—UNTIL LOSS OF HEALTH SHOWS IT!

Here's a CONCENTRATED SUPPLY of these 3 Vital Vitamins

VEGEMITE–a delicious extract of YEAST—

the richest food source of the combined vitamins B₁, B₂ and P.P.

Ask for VEGEMITE

the concentrated extract of YEAST

The richest combined source of these Vitamins B1, B2 and P.P.

Set for a stroll?

IN 1944 Wendy Gamble was a "happy little VEG·E·MITE"

AND NOW Wendy is a merry marching girl

...and still a VEGEMITE fan

All the family need delicious VEGEMITE every day

Always put VEGEMITE next to the pepper and salt whenever you set the table.

There's a rose in every...

Happy 'LITTLE VEG...

VEGEMITE is r... these 3 VITAM... your body can't...

B1 — for healthy nerves
B2 — for firm body tissues
Niacin — for good digestion and clear skin

Be a happy, healthier VEGEMITE family

PUT VEGEMI... NEXT TO THE P... AND SALT... ...EVE... BETT... TABL...

---

the VEGEMITE cookbook

...s a rose in
every cheek

of these happy
little triplets
Meija, Iowa and Zane...

Feeling Colourless?

Vegemite is rich in these 3 vitamins you need every day

VITAMIN B1

VITAMIN B2

NIACIN

very day kiddies

VEGEMITE

Vital...

IN 1953

Daryl Brown was a "happy little VEG-E-MITE"

AND NOW

Daryl is a sturdy Rover Scout...

...and still a VEGEMITE fan

All the family need delicious VEGEMITE every day

Who said vitamins were dull?

Boys will be boys.

VEGEMITE has long
been a household name,
promoted for its variety
of uses and recognised
for its iconic ads
over the years.

60s

If you can't beat 'em...

IT ISN'T
JUST FOR KIDS!
VEGEMITE

WHO SAID
VITAMINS WERE DULL?
VEGEMITE

← VEGEMITE's ads
later evolved to include
the yellow and red colours
now iconic to the brand.

11

Growing stronger with VEGEMITE every day

VEGEMITE IMPROVES YOUR FOREHAND AND BACKHAND.

THE VITAMIN B IN VEGEMITE™ PROMOTES GROWTH BY RELEASING THE ENERGY IN FOOD (AND TENNIS PLAYERS).

I'M STILL A VEGEMITE KID

I was always an energetic child, and VEGEMITE Yeast Extract played a leading role in keeping me going. It tastes great and it is great because it has those essential B Group Vitamins I need to carry me through a long filming session. You could say VEGEMITE Yeast Extract is a star in my life. That's why I'm still a VEGEMITE Kid.

VEGEMITE
A part of growing up you never outgrow

I'M STILL A VEGEMITE K

From the time the only driving I did was in a billy-cart, VEGEMITE Yeast Extract has been helping me over the rough spots. It tastes great and it is great, because it has those essential B Group Vitamins I need to stay ahead. VEGEMITE Yeast Extract helps me maintain my energy and concentration even on the toughest drive. I'm still revving with VEGEMITE. That's why I'll always be a VEGEMITE Kid.

VEGEMITE
A part of growing up you never outgrow

To encourage growth simply apply Vegemite.

Free Vegemite Growth Wall Chart Offer

AT JUST 3c A SERVE, VEGEMITE PUTS A ROSE IN EVERY CHEEK.

Some things never change. Kids love VEGEMITE

I'm still a Vegemite Kid

Vegemite helps

12   the VEGEMITE cookbook

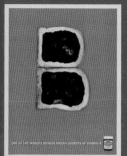

ONE OF THE WORLD'S RICHEST KNOWN SOURCES OF VITAMIN B

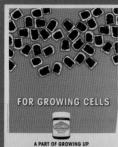

FOR GROWING CELLS

A PART OF GROWING UP

ONE OF THE WORLD'S RICHEST KNOWN SOURCES OF VITAMIN B

FOR A QUICK START.

BRIGHT AS
BRIGHT
CAN BE.

ONE OF THE WORLD'S RICHEST KNOWN SOURCES OF VITAMIN B

SQUEEZE IT
INTO YOUR
BACKPACK.

VEGEMITE
Comes of age

PUT A ROSE IN YOUR CHEEKS AND WIN A
TRUE BLUE AUSSIE FAMILY HOLIDAY!

Token 3

HOW TO WIN A RELAXING AUSSIE HOLIDAY!

VEGEMITE
Growing up with our nation

PUT A ROSE IN YOUR CHEEKS AND WIN A
TRUE BLUE AUSSIE FAMILY HOLIDAY!

Token 2

HOW TO WIN A RELAXING AUSSIE HOLIDAY!

2000s

YOU
DON'T
have to
STOP at
TOAST
when you

START
with

VEGEMITE
B VITAMINS
FOR VITALITY

HOW DO YOU LIKE
YOUR VEGEMITE?

'THE TIGER TOASTER'

HOWDOYOULIKEYOURVEGEMITE.COM.AU

HOW DO YOU LIKE
YOUR VEGEMITE?

THE DUNKER

HOWDOYOULIKEYOURVEGEMITE.COM.AU

HOW DO YOU LIKE
YOUR VEGEMITE?

THE RE◆BACK

HOWDOYOULIKEYOURVEGEMITE.COM.AU

HOW DO YOU LIKE
YOUR VEGEMITE?

THE VEGECADDER

HOWDOYOULIKEYOURVEGEMITE.COM.AU

HAPPY LITTLE VEGEMITES

Being part of the VEGEMITE family is as special as the spread itself and VEGEMITE would not be what it is today without the passion of its MITEY crew.

Barry Irvin

When did you start working at VEGEMITE and what is your role?
As the Executive Chairman of Bega Cheese I led the team that acquired VEGEMITE and brought the brand name back home in 2017.

Why do you love working at VEGEMITE? What's kept you here for so long?
In my case, being part of the team that was able to bring VEGEMITE back into Australian ownership was a great feeling. Seeing how wonderfully both new and old staff at VEGEMITE Way came together and continue to be so proud and positive about the company and the brand is inspiring.

FOR CHILDREN, TEENAGERS AND ADULTS VEGEMITE EVERYONE NEEDS IT DAILY

the VEGEMITE cookbook

What's your fondest memory of working at VEGEMITE?

The day that we were announcing the purchase of VEGEMITE I was walking down the road to the factory at Port Melbourne on my own and feeling a little nervous. I still remember the smell of VEGEMITE in the air and I smiled to myself thinking, *Well, I am definitely in the right place*. I told myself to remember this is a great day. I think my second was most recently when I was in the UK and one of our staff members was celebrating his 50th year with the business. Rob Carman is always such a positive presence at VEGEMITE Way and it was lovely, despite the time differences, to be able to give him a call, chat about some of his experiences over the years and say thank you to a wonderful employee.

What impact has VEGEMITE had on your life? Has it always been a big part of your life?

There is no more iconic brand in Australia than VEGEMITE. It has of course always been a part of my life from my earliest memories as a child, to singing along to Men At Work at the Tathra Pub in the early '80s as they belted out that line about a VEGEMITE sandwich from their hit 'Down Under', right through to being so proud of our association with Ash Barty and her wonderful approach to life, and her achievements. As far as impact is concerned, I think it is more that, for many Australians, VEGEMITE is always there, always makes you feel good, is great on toast for breakfast – there's nothing like some fresh white bread, butter and VEGEMITE – and these days adds a nice flavour to whatever you might be cooking. It is safe, convenient and evokes nice memories. No wonder it is loved.

'There's nothing like some fresh white bread, butter and VEGEMITE'

What's your earliest memory with VEGEMITE?

I suspect it is my primary school lunches. I would have obviously been eating it from a much younger age but my memory is of unwrapping the sandwich and eating it while drinking whatever flavoured milk had been delivered to the school through the old school milk programs (I'm really showing my age now!).

Sandra Dal Maso

When did you start working at VEGEMITE and what is your role?
February 1989. I am currently General Manager – Research and Development.
In this role I am responsible for the process, product and packaging for all our products, including VEGEMITE. I started out as a Packaging Technologist.

Why do you love working at VEGEMITE? What's kept you here for so long?
I love working on our unofficial national icon. Virtually everyone has a fond memory of VEGEMITE. People's faces light up when I tell them that I work at VEGEMITE and they usually tell me a story or anecdote. Very few jobs have such a positive impact. I love the fact that VEGEMITE is generational. Many people tell me how they grew up on VEGEMITE and now they are feeding it to their children and sometimes grandchildren.

What's your fondest memory of working at VEGEMITE?
We have run a lot of promotions over the years – we have launched collectible jars, special blend editions. I was part of the infamous iSnack 2.0 product launch. However, my fondest memory is of the campaign around the manufacture of the billionth jar. It is exciting to know that at VEGEMITE we have filled more than a billion jars, and those jars of VEGEMITE have been consumed in most Australian households, including those of all our family and friends.

What's your earliest memory with VEGEMITE?
I think my first exposure to VEGEMITE was in kindergarten. Coming from a migrant Italian household we did not have VEGEMITE when I was a toddler. But from kindergarten onwards, VEGEMITE was always around me, either in school lunches or at birthday parties. The VEGEMITE sandwiches were always on the party table next to the chocolate crackles and fairy bread.

There are as many different ways to consume VEGEMITE as there are people. Even a VEGEMITE sandwich can spark a significant debate about whether a person should apply a scraping of VEGEMITE or slather it on, butter or no butter, white bread or multigrain or sourdough or crackers or flatbread. I personally love VEGEMITE in my bolognese sauce. It provides great depth of flavour.

Rob Carman

'Growing up, we always had fresh buttered bread with VEGEMITE'

When did you start working at VEGEMITE and what is your role?
24 January 1972 (fifty years ago). My current role is Facility Manager.
I am responsible for all maintenance of the buildings and equipment in
the services department at the VEGEMITE plant. I started as an apprentice
fitter and turner. It was a four-year apprenticeship.

Why do you love working at VEGEMITE? What's kept you here for so long?
There are two things I love about working at VEGEMITE. The first is working
with the great team that actually makes and bottles VEGEMITE, who
are very passionate about their job. The second is being part of a
national icon in VEGEMITE.

What's your fondest memory of working at VEGEMITE?
I was very fortunate to have been part of previous VEGEMITE
celebrations, including a street party for the opening of VEGEMITE
Way. Also being part of TV footage for VEGEMITE's major milestones –
for example, its 70th, 80th and 90th birthdays, the manufacture of
the billionth jar and many more. Great memories!

**What impact has VEGEMITE had on your life? Has it always
been a big part of your life?**
I love VEGEMITE! Growing up, we always had fresh buttered bread with
VEGEMITE on the kitchen table for a snack. Working at the plant was
also a highlight. Part of my career was actually working in the VEGEMITE
department, being responsible for the maintenance of all the manufacturing
equipment.

What's your earliest memory with VEGEMITE?
Work functions where we'd listen to 'Happy Little VEGEMITEs' and girls would march
to the tune of the song. And VEGEMITE at kids' parties – on bread and in scrolls.
We still provide these for visitors at the plant today.

KIDS LOVE EATING VEGEMITE

Whether you've been introduced to VEGEMITE young or old, everyone has their own special views about VEGEMITE.

Flynn, 10 years old

How much do you love VEGEMITE?
A lot, because I like that it's made in Australia.

What's your favourite thing to eat VEGEMITE on or with? On toast.

What do you think VEGEMITE tastes like? Salty.

Do you have any advice you'd like to give VEGEMITE?
No, because it's perfect as it is!

What other products would you like to see VEGEMITE make? VEGEMITE popcorn.

Avery, 4 years old

How much do you love VEGEMITE? Five.

What's your favourite thing to eat VEGEMITE on or with? Toast toast toast.

What do you think VEGEMITE tastes like?
Orange. VEGEMITE tastes like jam.

Do you have any advice you'd like to give VEGEMITE? I love jam.

What other products would you like to see VEGEMITE make? No.

the VEGEMITE cookbook

Lottie, 6 years old

How much do you love VEGEMITE?
[Spreading her arms] So, so much.

What's your favourite thing to eat VEGEMITE on or with? On toast with avocado and ham.

What do you think VEGEMITE tastes like? VEGEMITE.

Do you have any advice you'd like to give VEGEMITE? They could make bigger jars.

What other products would you like to see VEGEMITE make? VEGEMITE spaghetti.

"Pass the VEGEMITE please Mum"

Growing stronger with Vegemite every day

Arlia, 7 years old

How much do you love VEGEMITE? That's a hard question. VEGEMITE is one of my favourite toppings on toast.

What's your favourite thing to eat VEGEMITE on or with? Toast.

What do you think VEGEMITE tastes like? It tastes a bit tingly when it's all by itself on my tongue.

Do you have any advice you'd like to give VEGEMITE? I love VEGEMITE.

What other products would you like to see VEGEMITE make? VEGEMITE cheese.

Heidi, 9 years old

How much do you love VEGEMITE? As big as the moon.

What's your favourite thing to eat VEGEMITE on or with? Cheesymite scrolls.

What do you think VEGEMITE tastes like? Like a tap dancer dancing on my tongue.

Do you have any advice you'd like to give VEGEMITE? Keep up the good work.

What other products would you like to see VEGEMITE make? VEGEMITE chocolate syrup.

Ivanka, 9 years old

How much do you love VEGEMITE? A lot!

What's your favourite thing to eat VEGEMITE on or with? Toast with butter and VEGEMITE.

What do you think VEGEMITE tastes like? Salty and YUM!

Do you have any advice you'd like to give VEGEMITE? I love VEGEMITE, I hope you make more VEGEMITE!

What other products would you like to see VEGEMITE make? Biscuits, chips, pasta.

Ava, 7 years old

How much do you love VEGEMITE? 2000 per cent GOOD!

What's your favourite thing to eat VEGEMITE on or with? Toast.

What do you think VEGEMITE tastes like? It tastes a bit salty and a bit sour-y. When I eat it, it has a bit too much salt and sour mixed together.

Do you have any advice you'd like to give VEGEMITE? You could make it a rainbow colour . . .

What other products would you like to see VEGEMITE make? VEGEMITE medicine to fix people's bodies.

Charlie, 12 years old

What's your favourite thing to eat VEGEMITE on or with? Toast!

What do you think VEGEMITE tastes like? It tastes likes Marmite on steroids.

Do you have any advice you'd like to give VEGEMITE? Cancel anyone on Twitter who does the VEGEMITE challenge.

What other products would you like to see VEGEMITE make? VEGEMITE cheese (preferably a brie).

the VEGEMITE cookbook

Year 2000 Limited Edition

The future is as bright as bright can be.

VEGEMITE
KRAFT

VEGEMITE
CONCENTRATED YEAST EXTRACT
KRAFT All Natural
455 g NET
PRODUCT OF AUSTRALIA

KIDS LOVE EATING VEGEMITE

21

TASTES LIKE AUSTRALIA

the VEGEMITE cookbook

HAPPY LITTLE VEGEMITEs

TASTES LIKE AUSTRALIA →

VEGEMITE

TASTES LIKE:
SWIMMING IN A FRIEND OF A FRIEND OF A FRIEND'S POOL

TASTES LIKE:
PUNCHING A SHARK IN THE FACE DURING A SURF COMP

TASTES LIKE:
BEING GIRT BY SEA

TASTES LIKE:
A BREAKFAST OF CHAMPIONS

TASTES LIKE:
WATCHING A 5 SETTER UNTIL 3AM

TASTES LIKE:
PERFECTING WHAT ENGLAND INVENTED

TASTES LIKE:
MAKING THE TASTIEST AUSSIE PIZZA EVER

TASTES LIKE:
TAKING A SPECCIE

TASTES LIKE:
HAVING A PUBLIC HOLIDAY FOR A HORSE RACE

TASTES LIKE:
EASY-PEASY VEGEMITE SQUEEZY

the VEGEMITE cookbook

BREAKFAST

VEGEMITE *with bacon*

VEGEMITE *with tomato and feta*

VEGEMITE *with avo*

VEGEMITE *with cheese*

VEGEMITE *with avo, egg and chives*

VEGEMITE with fried egg

VEGEMITE Toast Toppers

Kickstart your morning with **VEGEMITE**
and these delicious toast toppers.

VEGEMITE with fried egg

Spread sourdough toast with butter (optional) and **VEGEMITE**.
Top with fried egg and sprinkle with fresh thyme.

VEGEMITE with avo

Spread sourdough toast with butter (optional) and **VEGEMITE**.
Top with sliced avocado and garnish with parsley.

VEGEMITE with tomato and feta

Spread multigrain toast with butter (optional) and
VEGEMITE. Top with sliced tomato then sprinkle
with crumbled feta, and dried chilli flakes.

VEGEMITE with cheese

Spread wholemeal toast with butter (optional)
and **VEGEMITE**. Top with a slice of tasty cheese.

VEGEMITE with avo, egg and chives

Spread sourdough toast with **VEGEMITE**. Top with smashed
avocado, a fried egg and finely chopped chives.

VEGEMITE with bacon

Spread toast with butter (optional) and **VEGEMITE**
and top with cooked bacon.

VEGEMITE
Breakfast Pizza

PREP TIME: 10 mins

COOKING TIME: 15 mins

SERVES: 2

2 small pita breads (18–20 cm)

1 tablespoon **VEGEMITE**

1⅓ cups (135 g) grated pizza
cheese blend

2 eggs

60 g finely sliced or
shredded ham

6 cherry tomatoes, halved

handful of baby spinach
leaves, to garnish

The big Aussie brekkie – all on a pizza!

1. Preheat oven to 200°C/180°C fan-forced and lightly oil a large baking tray. Place the pita breads onto the tray.
2. Spread each pita bread with **VEGEMITE** then sprinkle with ⅓ of the cheese, making it into a slight nest shape to hold the eggs. Carefully break an egg onto each pita bread, then top with ham, cherry tomatoes and the remaining cheese.
3. Bake for 10–15 minutes or until the egg is cooked to your liking and the bread is crisp. Garnish with baby spinach and serve immediately.

the **VEGEMITE** cookbook

pizza
can be for
brekkie, too!

Poached Eggs with VEGEMITE & Smashed Avo

PREP TIME: 10 mins

COOKING TIME: 5 mins

SERVES: 2

1 avocado

2 tablespoons crumbled feta

2 eggs

2 slices sourdough bread,
    toasted

butter, for spreading

VEGEMITE, for spreading

fresh dill, to garnish

Everyone will gather around the breakfast table in no time when you start the day with **VEGEMITE**, poachies and smashed avo.

1. Place the avocado flesh and feta in a small bowl and mash together roughly with a fork.
2. Bring a saucepan of water to the boil. Reduce to a slight simmer and stir to create a whirlpool. Carefully break the eggs into the water. Cook for 3–4 minutes, or until the whites are set. Remove from the water with a slotted spoon and drain.
3. Spread the toast with butter and **VEGEMITE** and place onto serving plates. Top with the smashed avocado mixture and eggs. Season to taste, garnish with dill and serve immediately.

Boiled Egg & VEGEMITE Soldiers

PREP TIME: 5 mins

COOKING TIME: 5 mins

SERVES: 2

2 eggs

2 slices multigrain bread,
   toasted and buttered

2 teaspoons **VEGEMITE**

You'll have **HAPPY LITTLE VEGEMITE**s when you serve this updated classic at breakfast.

1. Place the eggs in a saucepan and add enough hot water to cover. Bring to the boil then reduce the heat slightly and simmer for 3 minutes, for soft yolks.

2. Spread the toast with **VEGEMITE** and cut into 2 cm fingers to make soldiers. Place the eggs into egg cups and slice off the tops. Dip the soldiers into the soft yolks.

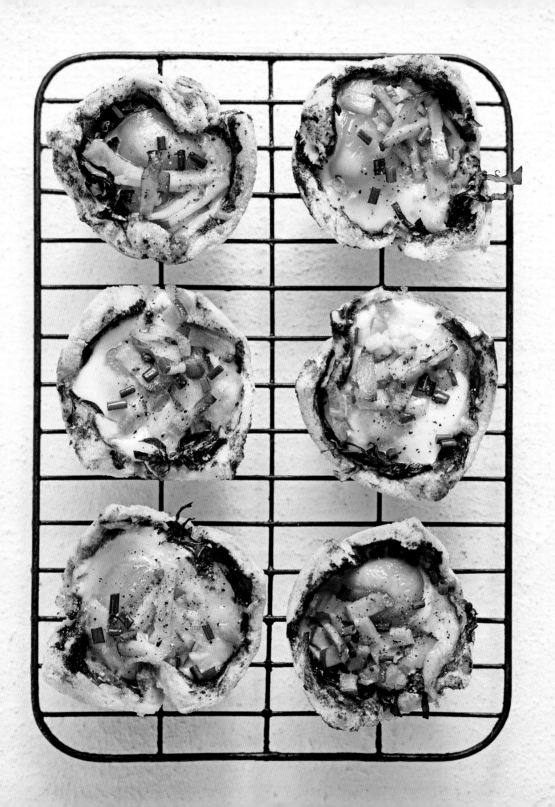

VEGEMITE Breakfast Muffins

Bake a batch of these tasty **VEGEMITE** muffins to give you and your family a delicious start to the day. These are also great for breakfast on the go or added to a lunchbox.

1. Preheat oven to 190°C/170°C fan-forced and brush a 6-hole large muffin tin with a little of the melted butter.
2. Flatten each bread slice with a rolling pin until very thin. Brush both sides of the bread with melted butter. Spread one side only with **VEGEMITE**. Press 1 slice of bread, with the **VEGEMITE** facing up, into each hole in the muffin tin.
3. Bake for 5 minutes or until the bread is slightly firm. Remove the tin from the oven and sprinkle spinach and cheese into each bread cup. Crack 1 egg into each cup. Season with freshly ground black pepper and top with the bacon.
4. Bake for a further 15 minutes or until the whites are set. Remove from the tin and sprinkle with the chives before serving.

PREP TIME: 10 mins
COOKING TIME: 20 mins
MAKES: 6

2 tablespoons butter, melted
6 slices white bread, crusts removed
1 tablespoon **VEGEMITE**
30 g finely chopped spinach
¼ cup (30 g) grated reduced-fat tasty cheese
6 eggs
2 tablespoons finely chopped raw bacon
1 tablespoon chopped chives

VEGEMITE BLT

PREP TIME: 10 mins

COOKING TIME: 6 mins

SERVES: 2

4 shortcut bacon rashers

4 slices sourdough bread

butter, for spreading (optional)

VEGEMITE, for spreading

2 leaves iceberg lettuce,
   shredded

1 large tomato, sliced

1 large avocado, sliced

Want the secret for the ultimate BLT?
Add **VEGEMITE** to elevate this iconic snack.

1. Cook the bacon in a non-stick frying pan for 2–3 minutes each side or until crisp and golden brown (add a little oil if necessary). Meanwhile, toast the bread.

2. Spread the toast with butter, if using, and **VEGEMITE**. Top 2 slices with the lettuce, tomato, bacon and avocado. Place the remaining toast slices on top. Serve immediately.

the **VEGEMITE** cookbook

VEGEMITE
Quesadilla

PREP TIME: 5 mins
COOKING TIME: 8 mins
SERVES: 1

olive oil spray

2 corn tortillas

2 teaspoons **VEGEMITE**

1 slice ham, chopped

¼ cup (30 g) grated tasty
cheese

¼ cup (65 g) tomato salsa

⅓ cup (60 g) of fresh, frozen
(thawed) or canned corn
kernels

2 tablespoons chopped
coriander, plus extra to serve

1 egg

chilli sauce (optional)

Filled with **VEGEMITE**, ham, cheese, salsa, corn
and coriander, and enveloped between two crispy
tortillas, this delicious quesadilla makes breakfast
easy. It's perfect for any day of the week.

1. Spray one side of each tortilla with a little of the oil, then
   spread **VEGEMITE** on the opposite side of one of the tortillas.
   Place it in a frying pan, **VEGEMITE** side up. Top with the ham,
   cheese, salsa, corn kernels and coriander, followed by the
   other tortilla, oiled side up.
2. Cook over medium heat for 4–5 minutes, turning once,
   until tortillas are crisp and golden and the cheese has melted.
   Transfer the quesadilla to a plate.
3. Heat the remaining oil in the pan and cook the egg to your
   liking. Place on top of the tortilla. Sprinkle with extra coriander
   and drizzle with chilli sauce, if using.

TIP: Omit ham to make a vegetarian quesadilla.

the **VEGEMITE** cookbook

why not mix things up in the morning!

Poached Eggs with Roast Tomatoes, Mushrooms & Spinach

Loaded with mushrooms, tomatoes, spinach and **VEGEMITE** and topped with a poached egg, this tasty weekend brekkie is always a crowd-pleaser.

1. Preheat oven to 220°C/200°C fan-forced and line a baking tray with baking paper.
2. Place the tomatoes onto prepared tray. Drizzle with the olive oil and vinegar, and season with salt and freshly ground black pepper. Roast for 10 minutes or until tomatoes just start to collapse. Set aside.
3. Melt 1 tablespoon butter in a frying pan. Add the spinach and cook, stirring often, until wilted. Transfer to a plate and set aside. Heat remaining butter in the pan and add the mushrooms. Cook, stirring occasionally, until soft and golden. Set aside.
4. Bring a saucepan of water to the boil. Reduce to a slight simmer and stir to create a whirlpool. Carefully break the eggs into the water. Cook for 3–4 minutes, or until the whites are set. Remove from the water with a slotted spoon and drain.
5. Spread the toast with **VEGEMITE** and place onto serving plates. Top with the poached eggs, and place the wilted spinach, cherry tomatoes and mushrooms alongside. Season to taste and serve immediately.

PREP TIME: 10 mins
COOKING TIME: 20 mins
SERVES: 2

250 g cherry tomatoes on the vine
1 tablespoon olive oil
1 tablespoon balsamic vinegar
2 tablespoons butter
50 g baby spinach
100 g button mushrooms, halved
2 eggs
2 slices sourdough bread, toasted and buttered
VEGEMITE, for spreading

VEGEMITE
Virgin Bloody Mary

PREP TIME: 3 mins

SERVES: 1

VEGEMITE, freshly ground
   black pepper and dried chilli
   flakes to garnish rim of glass
   (optional)
½ teaspoon **VEGEMITE**
1 dash Worcestershire sauce
2 dashes Tabasco sauce
1 tablespoon lemon juice
ice cubes
¾ cup (180 ml) tomato juice
1 celery stalk, to garnish

Try this Aussie take on the traditional Bloody Mary
for a sure-fire brunch hit.

1. Brush a little **VEGEMITE** around the rim of a tall glass and dip
   in the pepper and dried chilli flakes, if garnishing the glass.
2. Place ½ teaspoon **VEGEMITE**, Worcestershire sauce, Tabasco
   sauce and lemon juice in the glass. Stir well to combine.
3. Fill the glass with ice cubes and add the tomato juice.
   Season with salt and freshly ground black pepper to taste
   and serve garnished with the celery stalk.

TIP: Add 30 ml vodka for a **VEGEMITE** Bloody Mary.

the **VEGEMITE** *cookbook*

VEGEMITE & Cheese Biscuits

PREP TIME: 10 mins + 30 mins resting

COOKING TIME: 15 mins

MAKES: about 24

¾ cup (110 g) plain flour

2 tablespoons self-raising flour

100 g cold butter, chopped

½ cup (60 g) grated cheddar cheese

½ cup (40 g) finely grated parmesan

1 teaspoon **VEGEMITE**

1 tablespoon cold water

2 tablespoons sesame seeds

You will love the salty, savoury flavour **VEGEMITE** gives to these simple biscuits.

1. Place the flours, butter, cheddar cheese, half the parmesan and the **VEGEMITE** into a food processor. Pulse until the mixture resembles large breadcrumbs. Add the water and pulse until the mixture starts to come together.

2. Turn out onto a lightly floured work bench and gather the dough together. Roll into a 3.5 cm diameter log and roll in the sesame seeds. Wrap in baking paper and refrigerate for 30 minutes to rest.

3. Preheat the oven to 180°C/160°C fan-forced and line a baking tray with baking paper.

4. Cut the log into 1 cm slices and place onto the prepared tray. Sprinkle over the remaining parmesan. Bake for 15 minutes until golden.

5. Remove from the oven and leave to cool on the tray.

6. Store in an airtight container for 3–4 days.

TIP: The rolled dough can be made up to 1 week in advance and stored in the fridge, or frozen for 3 months. Cook from frozen, adding 5 extra minutes to the cooking time.

VEGEMITE
Scones

PREP TIME: 20 mins
COOKING TIME: 12 mins
MAKES: about 15

5 cups (750 g) self-raising flour
pinch salt
pinch cayenne pepper
120 g cold butter, chopped
2½ cups (300 g) grated tasty
   cheese
2 tablespoons **VEGEMITE**
540 ml milk, plus extra for
   brushing
extra butter and **VEGEMITE**,
   to serve

Fill your home with the smell of these delicious **VEGEMITE** scones.

1. Preheat the oven to 220°C/200°C fan-forced and grease 2 baking trays.
2. Place the flour, salt, cayenne and butter into a food processor. Pulse until the mixture resembles breadcrumbs. Tip the contents into a bowl and stir through half the cheese.
3. Whisk the **VEGEMITE** into the milk in a bowl. Use a knife to stir in enough of the milk mixture to the flour mixture to form a soft dough. Gather the dough together.
4. Turn out onto a lightly floured work bench and gently pat out to 2–2.5 cm thickness. Use a floured 7 cm cutter to cut out scones. Place onto the prepared trays, brush with a little milk and sprinkle over the remaining cheese.
5. Bake for 12 minutes or until golden brown. Serve warm with extra butter and **VEGEMITE**.

TIP: Freeze leftovers individually wrapped, for up to 2 months.

the **VEGEMITE** cookbook

these make a
swirly good
snack!

VEGEMITE Scrolls

Stuck for lunch box and snack ideas?
These scrumptious **VEGEMITE** savoury scrolls
are always a hit!

1. Preheat the oven to 220°C/200°C fan-forced and grease
   a baking tray.
2. Sift the flour and salt into a bowl then rub through the butter.
   Stir in enough milk to make a soft dough. Gather the dough
   together and turn out onto a lightly floured work bench and
   knead gently. Use a rolling pin to roll out to a 40 cm x 25 cm
   rectangle.
3. Spread the **VEGEMITE** over the dough then sprinkle over
   the cheese. Starting from a long side, roll up to enclose the
   cheese. Cut the roll into ten 4cm-wide pieces and place
   close together, cut side up, on prepared tray.
4. Brush with a little milk and bake for 15–20 minutes,
   until cooked and golden.

PREP TIME: 15 mins
COOKING TIME: 20 mins
MAKES: 10

3 cups (450 g) self-raising flour
pinch salt
50 g butter
1¼ cups (310 ml) milk,
   plus extra for brushing
1–2 tablespoons **VEGEMITE**
1⅔ cups (200 g) grated
   tasty cheese

Tartlets

PREP TIME: 15 mins
COOKING TIME: 20 mins
MAKES: 18

2 sheets frozen puff pastry,
  just thawed
1 tablespoon **VEGEMITE**
100 g firm ricotta, crumbled
1 egg
2 tablespoons finely grated
  parmesan
250 g mixed cherry tomatoes,
  sliced into 3
thyme leaves, to garnish

VEGEMITE adds a savoury twist to these delicious tartlets – perfect for a light lunch or tasty snack!

1. Preheat the oven to 210°C/190°C fan-forced and line 2 baking trays with baking paper.
2. Cut each sheet of pastry into 9 squares. Place onto the prepared trays, leaving space in between each piece. Use a knife to score a line around the edge of the pastry, 1 cm in from the sides, to create a border. Prick the base inside the border with a fork.
3. Bake for 8 minutes, until lightly golden. Remove from the oven, and using the back of a spoon, gently press down the centre of each square of pastry.
4. Mix the **VEGEMITE**, ricotta, egg and parmesan together in a small bowl until evenly combined.
5. Spread 2 teaspoons of ricotta mixture in the middle of each pastry square. Top with tomato slices.
6. Return the tarts to the oven to cook for 8–10 minutes or until golden.
7. Remove from the oven and garnish with thyme leaves and freshly ground black pepper. Cool on the trays for 5 minutes before serving.

Mini Curried Pasties

VEGEMITE adds a twist to these traditional pasties. Perfect for a light lunch with friends or as part of a party spread!

PREP TIME: 20 mins
COOKING TIME: 40 mins
MAKES: 12

1. Preheat the oven to 210°C/190°C fan-forced. Line 2 baking trays with baking paper.
2. Heat the oil in a frying pan over medium heat. Add the onion, curry and chilli powders, and cook for about 3 minutes, until soft. Add the lamb mince and cook, stirring and breaking up lumps with a wooden spoon, until lightly browned. Stir in the tomato and VEGEMITE, cook for 5 minutes, then add the potato.
3. Transfer the mixture to a large bowl and set aside to cool, stirring occasionally to release the heat (you can put the bowl in the fridge to cool faster).
4. Cut each sheet of pastry into 4 circles or squares. Place about ¼ cup of the meat mixture onto each pastry piece. Brush the edges of the pastry with water and fold over. Press the edges together with a fork to seal.
5. Place the pasties onto the prepared trays. Brush with beaten egg and bake for about 25 minutes or until the pastry is puffed and golden.
6. Meanwhile, make the mint raita. Grate the cucumber and place into a sieve. Press the cucumber to remove as much moisture as possible. Mix with the mint and yoghurt in a bowl. Serve with the pasties.

2 teaspoons olive oil
2 brown onions, chopped
2 teaspoons curry powder
1 teaspoon chilli powder
250 g lean lamb mince
1 tomato, chopped
1 tablespoon VEGEMITE
1 potato, diced and cooked
3 sheets frozen puff pastry, just thawed
1 egg, lightly beaten

Mint raita

1 Lebanese cucumber, halved lengthways, seeds removed
½ cup mint leaves, finely chopped
¾ cup (210 g) thick Greek-style yoghurt

Sausage Rolls

PREP TIME: 15 mins
COOKING TIME: 30 mins
MAKES: 16

2 tablespoons olive oil

1 brown onion, finely chopped

1 clove garlic, crushed

2 tablespoon fennel seeds

500 g lean pork mince

⅓ cup (25 g) panko
  breadcrumbs

2 eggs

2 sheets frozen puff pastry,
  just thawed

2 tablespoons **VEGEMITE**

2 tablespoons sesame seeds

tomato sauce, to serve

A tasty version of an Aussie classic. **VEGEMITE** gives an even more savoury flavour to these pork and fennel sausage rolls.

1. Preheat the oven to 180°C/160°C fan-forced. Line 2 baking trays with baking paper.

2. Heat the oil in a frying pan over medium heat. Cook the onion and garlic for about 3 minutes, until soft. Set aside until slightly cooled.

3. Place the fennel seeds and pork mince into a large bowl. Add the breadcrumbs, 1 egg and the cooked onion mixture. Season with salt and freshly ground black pepper.

4. Using a large spoon (or damp hands), mix all the ingredients together until well combined.

5. Cut each piece of pastry in half lengthways so you have 4 pieces. Spread each one with **VEGEMITE**. Take a quarter of the meat mixture and shape into a log down one long edge of a pastry piece. Repeat with the remaining meat and pastry.

6. Whisk the remaining egg in a small bowl. Brush the egg along the opposite edge of the pastry from the meat. Starting from the meat side, roll up the pastry pieces to enclose.

7. Cut each log into 4 pieces. Place the cut sausage rolls, seam side down, onto the prepared trays, leaving room to spread. Brush the tops of the sausage rolls with the remaining whisked egg and sprinkle with sesame seeds.

8. Bake for 20–25 minutes or until golden and cooked through. Cool for 5 minutes before serving with tomato sauce.

Salmon Cakes

PREP TIME: 20 mins
COOKING TIME: 15 mins
MAKES: 12

500 g skinless boneless salmon
    fillets, cut into 5 mm–1 cm
    pieces
3 spring onions, finely chopped
1 tablespoon finely grated
    ginger
2 teaspoons **VEGEMITE**
¼ cup coriander leaves
1 egg
1 teaspoon dried chilli flakes
¼ cup (50 g) rice flour
1½ cups (180 g) green beans,
    trimmed and thinly sliced
extra virgin olive oil, for cooking

Cucumber salad

¼ cup (60 ml) rice wine vinegar
1 teaspoon caster sugar
1 teaspoon **VEGEMITE**
½ teaspoon sesame oil
1 cucumber
¼ small red onion, finely sliced

A quick and easy way to add fish to your diet.
Add a dash of **VEGEMITE** to this traditional favourite
for an extra burst of flavour.

1. Place the salmon, spring onion, ginger, **VEGEMITE**, coriander, egg and chilli flakes into a food processor. Using the pulse button, process until the mixture just comes together. Transfer the mixture to a mixing bowl and stir through the rice flour and beans to combine well.

2. Heat a large frying pan over medium heat. Add enough oil to cover the bottom. Using a large ice-cream scoop or spoon (they will be about ¼ cup each), drop piles of mixture into the hot oil. Flatten slightly and cook for 2 minutes on each side, until golden and crisp. Remove from the oil and drain on paper towel. Repeat until all the mixture is used.

3. Meanwhile, make the cucumber salad. Whisk together the vinegar, sugar, **VEGEMITE** and sesame oil in a bowl. Use a peeler to cut the cucumber into long ribbons. Toss the cucumber and red onion in the dressing.

4. Place the salmon cakes onto serving plates with the cucumber salad. Serve immediately.

fresh and delicious!

Sweet Potato & Rosemary Pizza

PREP TIME: 10 mins

COOKING TIME: 40 mins

SERVES: 2

300 g sweet potato,
    scrubbed and sliced
    into 1 mm thick slices
garlic-flavoured olive oil spray
1 x 18–22 cm pizza base
1½ tablespoons **VEGEMITE**
2 whole rosemary sprigs
½ cup (50 g) grated pizza
    cheese blend or grated
    mozzarella

A good pizza needs a tasty base, which is where **VEGEMITE** comes in. Packed with flavour, these pizzas are sure to be a crowd-pleaser!

1. Preheat the oven to 200°C/180°C fan-forced. Line a baking tray with baking paper.
2. Place the sweet potato onto the prepared tray and spray with oil. Bake for 20–25 minutes or until just tender.
3. Place the pizza base onto a lightly oiled pizza tray and spread with **VEGEMITE**. Top with the sweet potato, rosemary and cheese. Bake for 10–15 minutes or until cooked through. Serve immediately.

Cheesy VEGEMITE Pizza

Who doesn't love **VEGEMITE** and cheese? A must-try delicious cheesy pizza that tastes like Australia!

1. Preheat the oven to 200°C/180°C fan-forced and lightly oil two pizza trays.
2. Place the pizza bases onto the prepared trays and spread with **VEGEMITE**, leaving some gaps without the spread.
3. Mix the butter, garlic and parsley in a small bowl until combined. Dollop the garlic butter into the gaps on the pizza bases and use the back of a spoon to spread it out.
4. Sprinkle evenly with the cheese and bake for 10–12 minutes, or until golden brown and bubbly. Remove from the oven and top with the prosciutto and rocket. Serve immediately.

PREP TIME: 10 mins
COOKING TIME: 12 mins
SERVES: 2–4

2 x 18–22 cm pizza bases
1 tablespoon **VEGEMITE**
20 g butter, softened
1 clove garlic, crushed
1 tablespoon finely chopped parsley
¾ cup (75 g) grated pizza cheese blend
4 slices prosciutto, thinly sliced
1 cup (30 g) baby rocket leaves

VEGEMITE
Noodles

PREP TIME: 10 mins
COOKING TIME: 10 mins
SERVES: 2

200 g dried egg noodles

¼ cup (30 g) frozen peas

1 cup (70 g) small broccoli florets

1 teaspoon vegetable oil

2 eggs

1 teaspoon **VEGEMITE**

1 large red or green chilli, thinly sliced

coriander sprigs, to serve (optional)

Quick and easy noodles with a **VEGEMITE** umami hit!

1. Cook the noodles in a large saucepan of boiling water according to the packet instructions, adding the peas and broccoli for the last 3 minutes of cooking.

2. Heat the oil in a frying pan over medium–high heat and fry the eggs until the whites are set and the yolks are cooked to your liking. Set aside.

3. Drain the noodle mixture, reserving ¼ cup (60 ml) of the cooking water. Return the noodle mixture to the pan, add the **VEGEMITE** and toss to combine.

4. Divide the noodle mixture between serving bowls. Top each with a fried egg and garnish with the chilli and coriander sprigs, if using.

VEGEMITE
Mac & Cheese

PREP TIME: 10 mins
COOKING TIME: 10 mins
SERVES: 4

500 g macaroni
2 tablespoons **VEGEMITE**
1 cup (120 g) grated tasty
   cheese
chopped chives, to garnish

An Aussie take on a classic. This one is sure to be a family favourite.

1. Cook the macaroni in a large saucepan of boiling water according to the packet instructions.
2. Drain the pasta, reserving ¼ cup (60 ml) of the cooking water. Return the pasta to the pan, then stir through the **VEGEMITE** and reserved water. Stir over low heat until the pasta is coated.
3. Add the grated cheese and stir to combine.
4. Remove from the heat and divide between 4 bowls. Garnish with the chives.

the **VEGEMITE** cookbook

next-level comfort food!

Beef Burgers

PREP TIME: 10 mins
COOKING TIME: 8 mins
SERVES: 4

500 g lean beef mince
2 tablespoons **VEGEMITE**
1 tablespoon olive oil
4 cheddar cheese slices
4 burger buns, split and toasted
mayonnaise, for spreading
cos lettuce leaves
2 tomatoes, sliced
½ red onion, finely sliced
tomato sauce

There's no need for takeaway when you can make these tasty burgers at home. A dash of **VEGEMITE** gives the patties an even richer flavour.

1. Combine the beef mince and **VEGEMITE** in a bowl and use damp hands to mix evenly. Divide into 4 equal portions and roll each into a ball. Press flat to form patties 9 cm in diameter.

2. Heat the oil in a frying pan over medium heat. Cook the burger patties for 3 minutes on each side.

3. Place a cheese slice on top of each patty and cook for a further 1–2 minutes, or until the cheese has started to melt.

4. Spread the burger bun bases with mayonnaise, and top each with a patty. Top with the lettuce, tomato, onion and tomato sauce and serve immediately.

Sure to be popular! ↓

Chicken Burgers

For a zesty twist on traditional chicken burgers, try marinating chicken fillets in **VEGEMITE**, sweet chilli and ginger. Delicious!

1. Combine the **VEGEMITE**, sweet chilli sauce and ginger in a bowl. Add the chicken thighs and turn to coat. Cover and marinate in the fridge for 30 minutes.
2. Heat the olive oil in a frying pan over medium–high heat. Cook the chicken for 5 minutes on each side or until cooked through. Transfer to a plate to rest for 5 minutes.
3. Meanwhile, toss the cabbage and carrot in a large mixing bowl. Combine the mayonnaise, yoghurt and mustard in a small bowl, then stir through the cabbage and carrot to coat well.
4. Place a chicken fillet onto the base of each bun and top with the coleslaw.

PREP TIME: 30 mins +
   30 mins marinating
COOKING TIME: 12 mins
SERVES: 4

1½ tablespoons **VEGEMITE**
⅓ cup (80 ml) sweet chilli sauce
5 cm piece ginger, finely grated
4 chicken thigh fillets
1 tablespoon olive oil
1½ cups (120 g) shredded cabbage
1 carrot, grated
1 tablespoon mayonnaise
1 tablespoon Greek-style yoghurt
1 teaspoon Dijon mustard
4 brioche burger buns, halved and toasted

Asian-style Chicken Slaw

PREP TIME: 15 mins
SERVES: 4

4 cups (320 g) finely shredded
   cabbage (wombok, red
   savoy)
3 carrots, finely sliced
4 spring onions, finely sliced
   on the diagonal
½ cup mint leaves
½ cup coriander leaves
2 cups (320 g) shredded
   cooked chicken
fried shallots and sliced fresh
   red chilli, to garnish (optional)

Dressing

1½ tablespoons rice wine
   vinegar
1 tablespoon honey
2 teaspoons **VEGEMITE**
1 clove garlic, crushed
1 tablespoon sesame oil

VEGEMITE gives a salty punch to this deliciously crunchy slaw.

1. To make the dressing, combine all the dressing ingredients in a screw-top jar. Seal tightly and shake well.
2. Toss the cabbage, carrots, spring onion, mint, coriander and chicken together in a large bowl.
3. Divide between 4 plates. Drizzle with the dressing and garnish with fried shallots and chilli, if using.

VEGEMITE
Bolognese

PREP TIME: 20 mins
COOKING TIME: 1 hour 10 mins
SERVES: 4

1 tablespoon olive oil
1 brown onion, finely chopped
2 cloves garlic, crushed
500 g lean beef mince
2 x 400 g cans chopped
   tomatoes or 700 g bottle
   passata
1 tablespoon **VEGEMITE**
2 teaspoons dried oregano
500 g spaghetti
finely grated parmesan,
   to serve
fresh parsley, to garnish

VEGEMITE makes for a rich and tasty addition to this family favourite. It's so good you'll want to make it a weekly staple.

1. Heat the olive oil in a large saucepan over medium heat and cook the onion and garlic for 5 minutes, until soft. Add the beef mince and cook, stirring and breaking up any lumps with a wooden spoon, until lightly browned.
2. Add the tomatoes, **VEGEMITE**, oregano and ½ cup (125 ml) water. Stir to combine. Cover and bring to the boil, then reduce heat to low and simmer gently for 1 hour.
3. When the sauce is almost ready, cook the spaghetti in a large saucepan of boiling water according to packet instructions, then drain.
4. Transfer the pasta to serving bowls and spoon over the bolognese. Toss to combine, and serve immediately with parmesan, freshly ground black pepper and garnish with parsley.

the **VEGEMITE** cookbook

VEGEMITE
Vegan Bolognese

Enjoy spaghetti bolognese with a plant-based twist using **VEGEMITE** for added depth of taste.

1. Heat the oil in a large saucepan over medium heat and cook the onion and garlic for 5 minutes or until soft. Increase heat to medium–high, add the mushrooms and cook until soft.

2. Stir in the tomato paste and cook, stirring, for 2 minutes. Add the tomatoes, lentils, **VEGEMITE** and large handful of parsley. Stir well and bring to the boil, then reduce heat to low and simmer gently, uncovered, for 15 minutes or until thickened.

3. When the sauce is almost ready, cook the spaghetti in a large saucepan of boiling water according to the packet directions. Drain.

4. Divide pasta between serving bowls and spoon over the sauce. Serve with vegan parmesan or yeast flakes, freshly ground black pepper and extra parsley.

TIP: The mushrooms can be chopped in a food processor.

PREP TIME: 15 mins
COOKING TIME: 30 mins
SERVES: 4–6

1 tablespoon olive oil
1 brown onion, finely chopped
2 cloves garlic, crushed
400 g Swiss brown or portobello
    mushrooms, finely chopped
2 tablespoons tomato paste
2 x 400 g cans cherry tomatoes
400 g can brown lentils, rinsed
    and drained
1 tablespoon **VEGEMITE**
large handful chopped
    parsley, plus extra to serve
500 g spaghetti
finely grated vegan parmesan
    or nutritional yeast flakes,
    to serve

Beef Pies

PREP TIME: 20 mins
COOKING TIME: 1 hour
MAKES: 6

1 tablespoon olive oil

2 bacon rashers, chopped

1 large brown onion, chopped

800 g lean beef mince

1 tablespoon plain flour

1 tablespoon **VEGEMITE**

1 carrot, grated

1 potato, grated

⅓ cup (70 g) tomato paste

large handful chopped parsley
   (optional)

5–6 sheets frozen puff pastry,
   just thawed

1 egg, lightly beaten

salad or steamed vegetables,
   to serve

VEGEMITE tomato sauce

2 teaspoons **VEGEMITE**

½ cup (125 ml) tomato sauce

Enjoy this classic that brings **VEGEMITE** into the mix.

1. Preheat the oven to 200°C/180°C fan-forced. Lightly grease a 13-cm (top measurement) six-holes pie tin.

2. Heat the oil in a large frying pan over medium heat. Cook the bacon and onion for 5 minutes or until the onion is soft. Increase heat to high, add the mince and cook, stirring and breaking up lumps with a wooden spoon, until browned.

3. Sprinkle the flour over the mince mixture. Add the **VEGEMITE**, carrot, potato, tomato paste and 1 cup (250 ml) water and stir to combine. Bring to the boil, reduce heat and simmer, covered, for 15 minutes or until thickened. Stir in parsley if using. Transfer to a large bowl and cool, stirring occasionally to release heat.

4. Place the **VEGEMITE** in a small bowl and gradually whisk in the tomato sauce. Set aside.

5. Cut around an upturned pie tin in the corner of a sheet of pastry to make a pastry lid. Repeat to make 6 lids. Use the remaining pastry to line the tins, trimming the pastry to fit and pressing overlapping edges gently to seal.

6. Fill the pastry-lined tins with beef mixture, cover with lids and press around the edges with a fork to seal. Brush pies with the egg and snip slits in the top of each pie with kitchen scissors.

7. Bake for 30–35 minutes, until pastry is deeply golden. Remove from the oven and allow to sit for 3 minutes before carefully sliding pies from tins. Serve with salad or vegetables, with VEGEMITE tomato sauce on the side.

nothing
beats a
warming pie
in winter

Chilli Con Carne

PREP TIME: 15 mins
COOKING TIME: 50 mins
SERVES: 4

1 tablespoon olive oil
1 brown onion, sliced
500 g lean beef mince
400 g can chopped tomatoes
400 g can red kidney beans,
    rinsed and drained
2 tablespoons **VEGEMITE**
2 tablespoons tomato paste
2 teaspoons ground cumin
½ teaspoon dried chilli flakes,
    or to taste
1 red chilli, sliced, to serve
steamed rice, to serve
large handful coriander leaves,
    to serve
lime wedges, to serve

Guacamole

2 avocado
pinch salt
juice of ½ lime
2 tablespoons finely
    chopped coriander

This tasty crowd-pleaser just got better with the addition of **VEGEMITE** for added depth and flavour. This recipe is a perfect mid-week meal or for casual get-togethers.

1. Heat the oil in a large saucepan over medium heat and cook onion for 5 minutes or until soft. Add the beef mince and cook, stirring and breaking up any lumps with a wooden spoon, until lightly browned.

2. Add the tomatoes, red kidney beans, **VEGEMITE**, tomato paste, cumin, chilli flakes and ⅓ cup (80 ml) water. Stir to combine. Bring to the boil then reduce the heat to low. Simmer gently, uncovered, for 20 minutes or until thickened and rich.

3. Make the guacamole close to serving time. Mash the avocado flesh with a fork or whisk in a bowl (don't overdo it as you want it to be chunky). Add salt, lime juice and coriander. Mix gently and set aside.

4. Serve the chilli con carne with rice, guacamole, fresh chilli, coriander leaves and lime wedges.

the **VEGEMITE** cookbook

Hearty Vegetable Soup

Warm your belly with this comforting soup made from fresh vegetables and pantry ingredients. The addition of **VEGEMITE** will put a rose in every cheek on a cold winter's day.

1. Heat the oil in a large saucepan over medium heat. Cook the leek, celery, carrot and garlic for 10 minutes, until softened.
2. Add the cabbage, zucchini and **VEGEMITE** and stir until combined. Stir in the stock and soup mix. Bring to the boil over high heat, then reduce the heat and simmer, partially covered, for about 2 hours or until the soup mix is tender and the soup has thickened. Extra water may be required if soup becomes too thick. Season well with freshly ground black pepper.
3. Sprinkle with the parsley, and serve with the crusty bread on the side.

TIP: For a speedier hearty soup, replace the dried soup mix with barley and cook for 1 hour until grains are tender.

PREP TIME: 20 mins
COOKING TIME: 2 hours 10 mins
SERVES: 4–6

1 tablespoon olive oil
2 leeks, thinly sliced
2 celery stalks, chopped
2 carrots, roughly chopped
2 cloves garlic, crushed
¼ cabbage (about 600 g), shredded
2 zucchini, chopped
2 tablespoons **VEGEMITE**
2 litres salt-reduced vegetable stock
1 cup (200 g) dried soup mix, well rinsed
handful chopped parsley, to garnish
crusty bread, to serve

Pumpkin & Sweet Potato Soup with VEGEMITE Croutons

PREP TIME: 20 mins
COOKING TIME: 20 mins
SERVES: 4

1 kg pumpkin, peeled and
    cut into 2 cm chunks
1 sweet potato, peeled and
    cut into 2 cm chunks
2 teaspoons **VEGEMITE**
3 cups (750 ml) salt-reduced
    vegetable stock, or water
120 g baby spinach leaves
1 tablespoon pepitas (optional)

VEGEMITE croutons

20 g butter
2 teaspoons **VEGEMITE**
1 tablespoon olive oil
3 thick slices sourdough bread
2 tablespoons finely grated
    parmesan

Make winter days golden with pumpkin, sweet potato and **VEGEMITE** in this deliciously velvety soup.

1. Preheat the oven to 180°C/160°C fan-forced.
2. Add the pumpkin, sweet potato, **VEGEMITE** and stock or water to a large saucepan. Bring to the boil over high heat, stirring until **VEGEMITE** has dissolved. Reduce the heat to medium and simmer uncovered, stirring occasionally, for 15 minutes or until the vegetables are tender.
3. Make the **VEGEMITE** croutons while the soup is cooking. Whisk the butter and **VEGEMITE** together in a saucepan, then add the oil and heat over low heat until melted and combined. Tear the bread into chunky 1.5 cm pieces and toss in the melted VEGEMITE mixture until combined.
4. Transfer to a baking tray, scatter with the parmesan and bake for 10–15 minutes, until crisp around the edges.
5. Remove the soup from the heat, cool slightly and blend until smooth. Reheat if necessary and stir in the spinach. Season well with freshly ground black pepper.
6. Ladle the soup into serving bowls and top with the croutons and pepitas if using.

the **VEGEMITE** *cookbook*

Shepherd's Pie

PREP TIME: 20 mins
COOKING TIME: 1 hour
SERVES: 4

1 tablespoon olive oil
1 brown onion, finely chopped
1 carrot, chopped
2 cloves garlic, crushed
500 g lean lamb mince
1 tablespoon tomato paste
200 ml salt-reduced beef stock
400 g can chopped tomatoes
2 tablespoons **VEGEMITE**
1 teaspoon gravy powder
1 cup (120 g) frozen peas
700 g mashing potatoes,
    peeled and chopped
    into 3 cm pieces
20 g butter
¼ cup (60 ml) milk
olive oil spray
steamed green beans,
    to serve

A universal favourite with a true blue Australian take. We've added **VEGEMITE** for extra richness and flavour.

1. Preheat the oven to 180°C/160°C fan-forced.
2. Heat the oil in a large frying pan over medium heat. Add the onion, carrot and garlic and cook for 5–7 minutes or until softened. Add the lamb mince and cook, stirring and breaking up any lumps with a wooden spoon, until well browned. Add the tomato paste and cook, stirring, for 2 minutes. Add the stock, tomatoes, **VEGEMITE** and gravy powder and stir until combined.
3. Bring to the boil over high heat, then reduce the heat to low and simmer for 20 minutes. Add peas and simmer for a further 5–10 minutes or until thickened.
4. While meat cooks, put the potatoes in a large saucepan and cover with cold water. Bring to the boil and cook for 15 minutes or until tender. Drain, then return the potatoes to pan. Mash well, then stir in the butter. Add the milk a little at a time, stirring until smooth.
5. Transfer the lamb mixture to a 2 litre baking dish. Spoon the mashed potato over the top, spray with olive oil and bake for 20 minutes or until bubbling and golden.
6. Remove from the oven and stand for 5 minutes, before serving with green beans.

the **VEGEMITE** *cookbook*

Barty Parmy

PREP TIME: 15 mins

COOKING TIME: 15–20 mins

SERVES: 1

1 small chicken breast fillet

¼ cup (35 g) plain flour

1 egg

¼ cup (20g) panko
    breadcrumbs

extra virgin olive oil,
    to shallow fry

2 tablespoons tomato
    pasta sauce

sliced ham, optional

½ cup (50 g) grated mozzarella

1 teaspoon **VEGEMITE**

TIP:
If you are
looking for a quick
and easy alternative,
try pre-crumbed oven-
bake schnitzels, which
you can buy from your
local supermarket
or butcher.

Have you ever wondered why England has an 'official' tennis dish (strawberries and cream) and yet Australia doesn't? Well, former World Number One, Grand Slam champion and proud Aussie Ash Barty believes the **VEGEMITE** Barty Parmy should be the unofficial official dish of Australian tennis. This Aussie pub classic is taken to an all-new level with **VEGEMITE**.

1. Preheat the oven to 200°C/180°C fan-forced and line a baking tray with baking paper.

2. Place the chicken breast between two sheets of baking paper and pound, using a meat mallet (or rolling pin), until about 2 cm thick.

3. Put the flour into a shallow bowl. Whisk the egg in a second shallow bowl, and spread the breadcrumbs into a third shallow bowl. Dip the chicken breast into the flour first, then the egg and finally the breadcrumbs, pressing on to coat evenly. Transfer to a clean plate and set aside.

4. Pour enough oil into a frypan to stand 3 mm deep. Heat oil over a medium-heat. When the oil is hot, cook the chicken for 3–4 minutes each side until golden brown and cooked through. Drain on paper towel then transfer to a baking tray.

5. Spoon pasta sauce over the chicken and top with the ham if using. Sprinkle on most of the mozzarella. Spread with **VEGEMITE** and finish with remaining cheese. Place in the oven and cook for about 5 minutes, until the cheese has melted. Serve with a simple side salad or vegetables.

TIP:
You can make
this recipe vegan
(swap the chicken breast,
egg and mozzarella for
vegan-friendly options)
vegetarian (swap the chicken
for a vegetarian option) or
gluten-free (use gluten free
bread crumbs and flour
and gluten-free
VEGEMITE)!

Roast Beef with VEGEMITE Gravy

VEGEMITE adds more richness to the humble roast. Jam-packed with flavour, it will become a Sunday special the whole family will enjoy.

1. Preheat the oven to 220°C/200°C fan-forced.
2. Heat a frying pan (or flameproof roasting pan) over high heat. Rub the oil over the beef and cook for 8 minutes, turning occasionally, until well browned all over.
3. Whisk the **VEGEMITE**, honey and pepper together in a small bowl and brush three-quarters of the glaze mixture over beef.
4. Place a rack into a roasting pan and sit the meat on the rack. Roast for 40 minutes, basting with the remaining glaze halfway through cooking, for medium result, or until cooked to your liking.
5. Remove from the oven and cover loosely with foil to rest for at least 15 minutes, while you make the quick gravy.
6. Melt the butter in a saucepan and scatter the flour over the top. Stir with a wooden spoon over low heat for 3–4 minutes, until lightly golden. Add the hot stock slowly, stirring constantly. Whisk in the **VEGEMITE** and sauces. Bring to a simmer and cook gently for 10 minutes, whisking occasionally, until thickened.
7. Carve the rested beef into thick slices and serve with vegetables and gravy.

TIP: Replace a portion of the stock in the gravy with pan resting juices if you have them.

PREP TIME: 15 mins
COOKING TIME: 1 hour 5 mins
SERVES: 6

2 teaspoons olive oil
1 kg beef roast (such as blade, sirloin or scotch roast, or 1.2 kg standing rib roast)
1 tablespoon **VEGEMITE**
1 tablespoon honey
¼ teaspoon freshly ground black pepper
steamed vegetables (baby carrots, green beans, peas, baby potatoes), to serve

Quick gravy

2 tablespoons unsalted butter
2 tablespoons plain flour
2 cups (500 ml) vegetable stock, heated
2 teaspoons **VEGEMITE**
1 tablespoon tomato sauce
1 teaspoon Worcestershire sauce

VEGEMITE-basted Lamb Loin Chops

PREP TIME: 20 mins + 30 mins standing

COOKING TIME: 10 mins

SERVES: 4

8 lamb loin chops or cutlets, trimmed

2 teaspoons **VEGEMITE**

2 teaspoons Dijon mustard

1 tablespoon maple syrup

olive oil cooking spray

2 baby cos lettuces, leaves separated

1 Lebanese cucumber, sliced

250 g cherry tomatoes, halved

shaved parmesan, to serve

Salad dressing

1 teaspoon **VEGEMITE**

1 teaspoon Dijon mustard

1 tablespoon olive oil

1 teaspoon balsamic vinegar

½ teaspoon caster sugar

It's hard to get more Australian than these succulent **VEGEMITE**-glazed lamb loin chops. A mouth-watering easy-to-make dinner the whole family will love.

1. Remove the lamb chops from the fridge 30 minutes before cooking. Whisk the **VEGEMITE** and mustard together in a small bowl, then gradually whisk in the maple syrup.

2. Spray the lamb chops lightly with oil. Heat a large frying pan, grill pan or barbecue over medium–high heat and cook the lamb for 2 minutes each side, then brush with the glaze and cook a further 1 minute each side or until caramelised and cooked to your liking.

3. Make the salad dressing while the lamb cooks. Whisk the **VEGEMITE** and mustard together in a small bowl, then gradually whisk in the oil, vinegar, sugar and 1 tablespoon water. Season with freshly ground black pepper.

4. Arrange the lettuce, cucumber and tomatoes in a salad bowl. Drizzle the dressing over the top and scatter with parmesan. Serve with the lamb chops.

Chicken Tray Bake

PREP TIME: 15 mins
COOKING TIME: 40 mins
SERVES: 4

8 medium or 4 large chicken
   thighs, bone in and skin on
200 g haloumi, cut into
   1.5 cm slices
2 lemons, halved
8 chat potatoes (500 g), halved
1 tablespoon **VEGEMITE**
1 tablespoon honey
2 sprigs rosemary
steamed broccolini, to serve

Make weeknight meals easier by cooking everything in one pan. This recipe is simple to prepare, requires minimal washing up, and the addition of **VEGEMITE** gives it maximum flavour.

1. Preheat the oven to 180°C/160°C fan-forced.
2. Place the chicken in a single layer in a large baking dish. Arrange the haloumi, lemons and potatoes around the chicken.
3. Whisk the **VEGEMITE** and honey together in a small jug, then gradually whisk in 1 tablespoon water. Pour over the chicken and scatter with rosemary.
4. Roast for 40 minutes or until golden and cooked through.
5. Serve with broccolini.

serve this and you'll have happy little VEGEMITES →

BBQ Pork Chops with Asian Slaw

PREP TIME: 20 mins + 30 standing
COOKING TIME: 10 mins
SERVES: 4

4 pork loin chops, trimmed
2 teaspoons **VEGEMITE**
1 tablespoon honey
1 tablespoon rice wine vinegar
2 teaspoons vegetable or
   peanut oil

Asian slaw

2 teaspoons **VEGEMITE**
2 teaspoons Dijon mustard
2 tablespoons maple syrup
2 tablespoons rice wine
   vinegar
½ wombok (Chinese)
   cabbage (about 500 g),
   finely shredded
1 red capsicum, finely sliced
1 carrot, shredded
large handful mint leaves
2 tablespoons roasted peanuts,
   roughly chopped

Perfect pork chops made even more so with the addition of **VEGEMITE**, which also adds an umami hit to this sensational slaw.

1. Remove the pork chops from the fridge 30 minutes before cooking. Whisk the **VEGEMITE** and honey together in a bowl, then whisk in the vinegar.

2. Drizzle the pork chops with the oil. Heat a barbecue, grill pan or large frying pan over medium–high heat. Cook the chops for 3 minutes each side, then brush with the glaze mixture and cook for a further 1 minute each side or until caramelised and cooked to your liking. Remove and set aside to rest for 5 minutes.

3. Make the Asian slaw while the chops are cooking. Whisk the **VEGEMITE** and mustard together in a small bowl. Gradually add the maple syrup and vinegar and whisk until combined. Combine the wombok, capsicum, carrot and mint in a large bowl. Scatter with the peanuts.

4. Serve the pork with the slaw, and the dressing on the side.

the **VEGEMITE** *cookbook*

Glazed Chicken Drumsticks

These lip-smackingly good sticky chicken drumsticks are ideal party food, great for munching on while watching the footy, and delicious served with coleslaw.

1. Make the marinade by whisking the **VEGEMITE**, honey and oil together in a large bowl. Add the chicken and toss to coat. Cover and place in the fridge for up to 2 hours.
2. Preheat the oven to 180°C/160°C fan-forced. Line a baking tray with baking paper.
3. Place the drumsticks in a single layer on the prepared tray. Bake for 20 minutes. Baste with pan juices and continue to cook for 15–20 minutes until golden and cooked through.
4. Combine the cabbage, carrot and spring onion in a large bowl. Combine the mayonnaise, yoghurt, lemon juice and 1 tablespoon cold water in an empty **VEGEMITE** screw-top jar and shake well. Pour over the cabbage mixture and toss to combine.
5. Divide the chicken between serving plates. Sprinkle with the sesame seeds and serve with the coleslaw.

PREP TIME: 10 mins + 2 hours marinating
COOKING TIME: 40 mins
SERVES: 4

8 chicken drumsticks
2 cups (160 g) finely shredded cabbage
2 carrots, finely shredded or thinly sliced
4 spring onions, finely sliced
1 tablespoon mayonnaise
1 tablespoon Greek-style yoghurt
1 tablespoon lemon juice
toasted sesame seeds, to serve

Marinade

3 tablespoons **VEGEMITE**
2 tablespoons honey
2 teaspoons olive oil

Fish with VEGEMITE Crumb Crust

PREP TIME: 15 mins
COOKING TIME: 15 mins
SERVES: 4

4 slices sourdough bread

⅓ cup (25 g) finely grated parmesan

1 tablespoon **VEGEMITE**

1 tablespoon butter

large handful parsley leaves, chopped

4 rockling fillets or any other thick firm white fish

250 g cherry tomatoes on the vine

steamed broccolini and rice, to serve

White fish fillets topped with a **VEGEMITE**–parmesan crumb will become your new favourite fish dish, guaranteed.

1. Preheat the oven to 200°C/180°C fan-forced. Line a baking tray with baking paper.
2. Cut off and discard most of the bread crusts. Blend or process the bread to make coarse breadcrumbs. Add the parmesan, **VEGEMITE**, butter and parsley and blend briefly until just combined.
3. Place the fish onto the prepared tray and press the crumb mixture onto each piece. Add the tomatoes to the tray.
4. Bake for 12–15 minutes or until the fish is cooked through and the crust is slightly coloured.
5. Serve the fish with the tomatoes, broccolini and rice.

the VEGEMITE cookbook

Prawn Hokkien Noodles

PREP TIME: 25 mins
COOKING TIME: 10 mins
SERVES: 4

450 g Hokkien noodles
1 tablespoon vegetable
 or peanut oil
250 g peeled raw pawns
2 cloves garlic, thinly sliced
2 teaspoons finely grated
 ginger
4 spring onions, white and
 green parts cut into
 3 cm lengths
1 bunch baby bok choy,
 stems and leaves roughly
 chopped separately
large handful coriander,
 stems and leaves chopped
 separately
1 red capsicum, sliced
100 g snow peas, trimmed

VEGEMITE stir-fry sauce

1 tablespoon **VEGEMITE**
⅓ cup (80 ml) sweet chilli sauce

You can't go past Hokkien noodles for a quick and easy dinner. Enjoy a bowl of these tasty noodles and the delicious umami hit that **VEGEMITE** gives to the sauce.

1. Make the **VEGEMITE** stir-fry sauce first. Gradually whisk 2 tablespoons water into the **VEGEMITE** in a small bowl, then whisk in the sweet chilli sauce.
2. Place the noodles into a large heatproof bowl and cover with boiling water. Stand for 3 minutes. Use a chopstick or fork to gently separate the noodles, then drain well.
3. Heat 2 teaspoons of the oil in a large wok or non-stick frying pan over high heat. Add the prawns and 1 tablespoon of the sauce and stir-fry for 2 minutes or until prawns change colour. Add the garlic and ginger and cook for a further minute or until fragrant. Transfer the prawns to a plate and set aside.
4. Add the remaining oil to the wok or pan and add the white spring onion sections, bok choy stems, coriander stems, capsicum and snow peas. Stir-fry for 3 minutes or until lightly charred. Add the drained noodles and the remaining spring onion, bok choy leaves and sauce. Return the prawns to the wok and stir-fry for 2–3 minutes or until they are heated through and the sauce coats the noodles.
5. Serve immediately, scattered with the remaining coriander.

the **VEGEMITE** *cookbook*

full of
fresh flavours

Tofu & Basil Stir-fry

This delicious **VEGE**tarian stir-fry is packed with flavour and will be on the table in less time than it takes to order takeaway.

PREP TIME: 10 mins
COOKING TIME: 10 mins
SERVES: 4

1. Heat a large wok or frying pan over high heat. Add the oil and tofu and stir-fry for 5 minutes until starting to colour. Add the garlic, ginger, chilli and beans. Stir-fry for 3 minutes until fragrant.
2. Mix the rice wine vinegar, honey and **VEGEMITE** together in a small jug.
3. Pour the mixture over the tofu in the wok and cook for a further 2 minutes, until the sauce is slightly thickened and coating the ingredients.
4. Stir in the cashews and basil. Divide between 4 bowls and serve with rice.

2 tablespoons vegetable oil

500 g firm tofu, roughly crumbled

2 cloves garlic, crushed

1 tablespoon finely grated ginger

2 long red chillies, seeds removed, roughly chopped

200 g green beans, cut into 4 cm pieces

1½ tablespoons rice wine vinegar

1 tablespoon honey

3 teaspoons **VEGEMITE**

Thai basil leaves, 1 bunch, picked

¼ cup (40 g) roasted unsalted cashews

steamed jasmine rice, to serve

Chocolate Raspberry Brownies

PREP TIME: 20 mins + cooling
COOKING TIME: 40 mins
MAKES: 15-18

300 g dark chocolate,
  chopped
2 tablespoons **VEGEMITE**
300 g unsalted butter
1½ cups (330 g) brown sugar
6 large (59 g) eggs, at room
  temperature
¾ cup (110 g) plain flour
⅓ cup (75 g) cocoa powder
1 teaspoon baking powder
250 g block cream cheese,
  softened
¾ cup (165 g) caster sugar
2 teaspoons vanilla bean paste
250 g raspberries (fresh
  or frozen)

VEGEMITE adds a slight saltiness to this sweet classic brownie recipe.

1. Preheat the oven to 180°C/160°C fan-forced. Line base of a 20 cm x 30 cm baking tin with baking paper, extending over the two long sides.

2. Melt the chocolate in a heatproof bowl in the microwave or over a double boiler and set aside to cool. Stir in the **VEGEMITE**.

3. Beat the butter and brown sugar together using an electric mixer until thick and pale. Add 4 of the eggs, one at a time, beating well between each addition. Sift the flour, cocoa and baking powder over the mixture and fold through until combined, then fold in the chocolate mixture.

4. Place the cream cheese, caster sugar, remaining 2 eggs and vanilla into a clean bowl and use the electric mixer to beat until smooth and creamy. Gently fold the cream cheese mixture into the chocolate mixture. Don't overwork the mixture – you're aiming for a marbled look.

5. Spoon the brownie mixture into the prepared tin and scatter over the raspberries. Bake for 40 minutes, until just set with a slight wobble in the centre.

6. Cool in the tin for 15 minutes. Lift out and cool completely on a wire rack. Cut into 15–18 pieces to serve.

the **VEGEMITE** *cookbook*

you have to try these! →

Lamingtons

An Aussie classic, made unexpectedly delicious with **VEGEMITE**.

1. Preheat the oven to 180°C/160°C fan-forced. Line the base of a 20 cm x 30 cm baking tin with baking paper.
2. Beat the butter, sugar, **VEGEMITE** and vanilla together with an electric mixer until light and fluffy. Add the eggs one at a time, beating well between each addition. Fold in the flour and buttermilk or milk alternately, about half at a time. Stir until just smooth.
3. Spoon mixture into a prepared tin and smooth into corners. Bake for 30–35 minutes or until a skewer inserted into the centre comes out clean.
4. Cool for 10 minutes in tin, then turn onto wire rack to cool completely.
5. Cut the cake in half horizontally and spread base with jam. Replace top and cut into 16 pieces.
6. Make the glaze by stirring milk and chocolate in medium saucepan over low heat until chocolate is melted. Remove from heat and whisk in **VEGEMITE** then icing sugar until smooth.
7. Working with 1 piece of cake at a time, dip the base into the glaze then place on a large fork held over the glaze. With the other hand, spoon glaze over the cake to coat. Allow excess glaze to drip off the cake, then coat each side in coconut.
8. Place onto a wire rack to set. Repeat with remaining cake and glaze. If glaze starts to thicken, warm gently over low heat.

TIP: For crumb-free dipping, freeze cake pieces for 1–1½ hours on a tray before coating.

PREP TIME: 60 mins + cooling
COOKING TIME: 35 mins
MAKES: 16

250 g unsalted butter, chopped
1 cup (220 g) caster sugar
2 teaspoons **VEGEMITE**
2 teaspoons vanilla bean paste
4 large (59 g) eggs, at room temperature
2 cups (300 g) self-raising flour, sifted
⅓ cup (80 ml) buttermilk or milk
½ cup (160 g) raspberry jam
3½ cups (260 g) shredded coconut

Chocolate VEGEMITE glaze

⅔ cup (160 ml) milk
100 g dark chocolate, chopped
1 tablespoon **VEGEMITE**
2 cups (320 g) soft icing mixture, sifted

VEGEMITE Cheesecake

PREP TIME: 30 mins + chilling
COOKING TIME: 1 hour + chilling
SERVES: 8–10

250 g plain sweet biscuits
150 g unsalted butter, melted
500 g cream cheese, at room
temperature, chopped
300 ml sour cream, at room
temperature
¾ cup (165 g) caster sugar
2 tablespoons **VEGEMITE**
1 teaspoon vanilla extract
2 large (59 g) eggs, at room
temperature
2 tablespoons plain flour
250 g mixed berries, to serve

Who doesn't love the melting, mouth-watering richness of a cheesecake? **VEGEMITE** adds a subtly salty touch that will make it hard to stop at just one piece.

1. Preheat the oven to 150°C/130°C fan-forced. Line the base of a 20 cm springform tin with baking paper.

2. Place the biscuits into a food processor and process until they resemble fine breadcrumbs. Add the butter and process until well combined.

3. Tip the biscuit mixture into the prepared tin, and using the back of a spoon evenly press the crumbs over the base and up the side of the tin, leaving a 1 cm gap around the top of the tin. Refrigerate for 30 minutes.

4. Clean out the food processor. Add the cream cheese, sour cream, sugar, **VEGEMITE** and vanilla. Process until combined. Scrape down the sides, add the eggs and flour, and process again until evenly combined.

5. Pour the filling into the crust. Sit the tin on a baking tray and place onto the middle shelf in the oven. Bake for 45 minutes, without opening the door, until cheesecake is set but still has a slight wobble in the centre. Turn the oven off and leave the cheesecake to cool for 2 hours in the oven with the door slightly ajar. Transfer to a wire rack and cool for 1 hour more at room temperature.

6. Refrigerate for 4 hours or overnight. Remove from the fridge and bring to room temperature before serving. Serve topped with the berries.

would like to thank everyone who has
worked on getting us to where we are today.

We would also like to extend a huge thanks to
our MITEY community— thank you for enjoying
VEGEMITE across breakfast, lunch and tea,
for singing our tune and for sharing us
with your friends and family.

It's been a MITEY 100 years and
we can't wait for 100 MITEY more!

Index

the VEGEMITE cookbook

TASTE

AUST

S LIKE

RALIA

PENGUIN BOOKS

UK | USA | Canada | Ireland | Australia
India | New Zealand | South Africa | China

Penguin Books is part of the Penguin Random House group of companies
whose addresses can be found at global.penguinrandomhouse.com

Penguin
Random House
Australia

First published by Penguin Books in 2022

Recipe development and food styling by Peta Gray
Recipe photography by Brent Parker Jones
Cover photography © Bega Cheese Limited
Cover and internal design by Adam Laszczuk © Penguin Random House Australia Pty Ltd
Typeset by Post Pre-press, Australia

Printed and bound in China by RR Donnelley

NATIONAL
LIBRARY
OF AUSTRALIA

A catalogue record for this
book is available from the
National Library of Australia

ISBN 978 0 14377 930 8

penguin.com.au

We at Penguin Random House Australia acknowledge that Aboriginal and Torres Strait Islander
peoples are the Traditional Custodians and the first storytellers of the lands on which we live
and work. We honour Aboriginal and Torres Strait Islander peoples' continuous connection
to Country, waters, skies and communities. We celebrate Aboriginal and Torres Strait Islander
stories, traditions and living cultures; and we pay our respects to Elders past and present.